Ripe Life

BOOKS IN THE PROTESTANT PULPIT EXCHANGE

Ripe Life

Sermons on the
Fruit of the Spirit

C. Thomas Hilton

PROTESTANT
PULPIT
EXCHANGE

Abingdon Press
Nashville

RIPE LIFE: SERMONS ON THE FRUIT OF THE SPIRIT

Library of Congress Cataloging-in-Publication Data

Hilton, C. Thomas (Clifford Thomas)
   Ripe life : sermons on the fruit of the Spirit / C. Thomas Hilton
     p.   cm. — (Protestant pulpit exchange)
   ISBN 0-687-38004-9 (alk. paper)
   1. Fruit of the Spirit—Sermons.   2. Sermons, American.
I. Title. II. Series.
BV4501.2.H485   1993
234'.13—dc20
                                          92-41993
                                          CIP

Scripture quotations, unless otherwise indicated, are from the New Revised Standard Version Bible, copyright © 1989, by the Division of Christian Education of the National Council of the Churches of Christ in the United States of America.

Scripture quotations noted GNB are from the *Good News Bible*—Old Testament: Copyright © American Bible Society 1976; New Testament: Copyright © American Bible Society 1966, 1971, 1976. Used by permission.

MANUFACTURED IN THE UNITED STATES OF AMERICA

For our four children
who taught me the significance
of the fruit of the Spirit:

Lynn,

Jean,

Karin,

Tom, Jr.

Contents

CONTENTS

Guided by the Spirit

How do I know when I am making spiritual progress in my life? Is there any objective criterion that can be applied? Am I a better person for being a Christian, or does it make any difference? Am I growing in grace? Am I improving? Just where do I measure on the spiritual scale?

These and similar questions are the ones I hear from the people in the congregation and from my own heart. Does the Bible offer any criteria for evaluating my life in the Spirit? Or is the answer the one my parents gave me when I inquired how I would know when I was really in love. "You'll know," they agreed, "You'll know."

For over fifty years I have been in love with God through Jesus Christ and I still entertain these kinds of questions. Preaching this series of sermons in a local congregation helped me to realize that there are in fact certain observable fruit of the Spirit. The challenge then became, how to ripen the fruit.

This series of sermons is based on the struggle with the nine fruit of the Spirit that the Apostle Paul shared with the church in Galatians 5:22. It is a struggle that every church and every Christian goes through. It is a struggle that Paul went through himself.

Paul, writing to the church in Rome said, "You are not in the flesh; you are in the Spirit, since the Spirit of God dwells in you" (Romans 8:9). The Church of Jesus Christ was in the Spirit, and hence these nine fruit should be found in abundance. This is the harvest that comes from living the abundant life.

The nine fruit of the Spirit are called by different names in different translations. While my basic translation for quotation is the New Revised Standard Version, I have based this listing on the Good News Bible (GNB) translation of Galatians 5:22:

"If we live by the Spirit," wrote Paul, "let us also be guided by the Spirit" (Galatians 5:25). Here is my attempt to be guided by the Holy Spirit. You will have to decide if I live by it.

C. Thomas Hilton
Interim Senior Pastor
Wayne Presbyterian Church
Wayne, Pennsylvania

> *Let love be genuine; hate what is evil, hold fast*
> *to what is good; love one another with mutual*
> *affection; outdo one another in showing honor.*
> *Romans 12:9*

Love

It comes as no surprise that love is the first fruit of the Spirit mentioned by the Apostle Paul in his listing of the nine spiritual crops to be harvested by the Holy Spirit in the life of a Christian. As a way to sum up, I John 4:8 tells us that "God is love." In reality, this is the only spiritual fruit, for all the others are derivatives. All the others are but added colors in the rainbow of love. Each of the other eight spell out more clearly the variety of this one manifestation of the presence of the Spirit in the life of the believer.

When the God of love dwells in your life, you will have joy, peace, patience, kindness, goodness, faithfulness, humility, and self-control (GNB). Paul details to the church in Galatians 5 the many works of the flesh, and when he finishes he hasn't really finished, for he concludes, "and things like that." In other words, there were many more "works of the flesh" that he could have mentioned, but did not. But when it came to detailing the presence of the Spirit in the life of the believer, it is one fruit—singular. The fruit involves one harvest of the Holy Spirit, giving a unified and cohesive character to what the Spirit produces in the Christian life.

Paul wanted the Galatians to understand this point clearly, for he wrote elsewhere in this letter, "Do not be deceived; God is not mocked, for you reap whatever you sow. If you sow to your own flesh, you will reap corruption from the flesh; but if you sow to the Spirit, you will reap eternal life from the Spirit." There it is in black and white. "So," he wrote, "let us not grow weary in doing what is right, for we will reap at harvest-time, if we do not give up" (6:7-9). What we will reap at harvest time is a crop of love, the specifics of which are spelled out in the expressions of love in the rest of Galatians 5:22. Again, Paul wrote to another church, "God's love has been poured into our hearts through the Holy Spirit that has been given to us" (Romans 5:5). We begin with love, for God is love and if, in fact, we desire to be godlike, then we shall embrace love. If, in fact, we are to follow the Christ about whom Paul preaches, we must be loving ourselves, as Jesus was loving. Paul calls this attitude, in his introduction to I Corinthians 13 (the love chapter), "a more excellent way."

But for all his talk about love (and the necessity for it), for all his efforts to persuade the early Christians to be Christlike, for all his attempts to model love for the early Church, Paul was not too successful. Our text has Paul admonishing the early Christians to have "genuine love." What other kind is there, we might ask? Why would he speak of genuine love, if he did not find much of the opposite in the Church?

Our text would indicate that Paul was struggling with a quality of love in the Church that left something to be desired. When you look at the evidence from other passages of Scripture, this would appear to be true.

First Peter, written from Rome to those having oversight of the churches in Asia Minor, speaks about "the genuineness of your faith," and "the genuine mutual love" that is needed. Again, there must be a fair amount of ingenuine faith present, in order to keep contrasting it to the genuine kind that these apostles desired.

I think we can safely say that Paul was having trouble growing genuine faith in the hearts of the believers. His letter to the church at Philippi (2:20) speaks about Timothy and how Paul will soon be sending him to them. Then he adds this revelation, "I have no one like him who will be genuinely concerned for your welfare. All of them are seeking their own interests, not those of Jesus Christ." All of them are? All but Timothy? If that's true, then there aren't many Spirit-filled Christians around. All of them? Really?

Writing to the church in Corinth, he twice mentioned the need for genuineness, speaking one time of the possibility of their taking an offering and adding, "I do not say this as a command, but I am testing the genuineness of your love against the earnestness of others" (II Corinthians 8:8). If he knew that they had genuine faith, he would not have to compare it to others. He would know. But he has to continually test the sincerity of the church members. Will they measure up or not? Are they genuine Christians or not? Have they caught the genuine love, or the ingenuine love? "Indeed, there have to be factions among you, for only so will it become clear who among you are genuine" (I Corinthians 11:19). Paul was having such difficulty that J. B. Phillips titles the twelfth chapter of Romans, "Let Us Have Real Christian Behavior," as if this were a scarce commodity.

I shouldn't imply that Jesus didn't face many of the same difficulties, for in his Sermon on the Mount, he said, "You hypocrite, first take the log out of your own eye, and then you will see clearly to take the speck out of your neighbor's eye" (Matthew 7:5). He also preached, "Beware of false prophets, who come to you in sheep's clothing but inwardly are ravenous wolves. You will know them by their fruits. Are grapes gathered from thorns, or figs from thistles? In the same way, every good tree bears good fruit, but the bad tree bears bad fruit. A good tree cannot bear bad fruit, nor can a bad tree bear good fruit. Every tree that does not bear good fruit is cut down and thrown into the fire." (Matthew 7:15-20).

> *"Ingenuine Love Is Selfish."*

What is genuine love and what is not? Our danger is that we become discouraged over the obvious evidence of so much lack of real love. I read where an instructor said to a new parachute trainee, "When you jump, the rip cord will pull automatically, but if it doesn't, pull the auxiliary chute on your back. If that doesn't work, pull the emergency cord. If that doesn't work—well, there will be an ambulance waiting for you on the ground." So the trainee jumped and nothing happened. He pulled the auxiliary cord and still nothing happened. He pulled the emergency cord. Nothing happened. He said, "Of all the luck! I suppose the ambulance won't be there either!" His pessimism was warranted—ours is not. But we ought to at least be realistic. Love was not overflowing in the biblical world, or even in the early Church. For many the ambulance wasn't even there to help bind up their wounds when their lives crashed.

Ingenuine love is easy to discern, for it is limited. It is guarded. It is a love that is conditional. I will love you, if you will love me in return. If you will do this for me, I will do that for you. It often involved bargaining. The one characteristic that is most obvious in ingenuine love in the Church is that it is selfish. Any expression of affection that is only self-serving is "erotic"; *eros* love, an expression of love for oneself. No matter what you called it, no matter how you dressed it up, no matter what others think it is, if it is motivated by a desire to serve one's own needs, it is ingenuine love.

Genuine love, *agape*, is expressed in the willingness of a person to lay down one's life for another. There is no greater love: "No one has greater love than this, to lay down one's life for one's friends" (John 15:13). This is the love that Christ models for us.

I read about an expression of genuine sacrificial love in Hollywood, Florida. A four-year-old child wanted to see the week-old puppies in her friend's backyard next door. Diana, 15, knew her dogs didn't like strangers, but she thought it would be all right if she accompanied Bernice into the yard, just to take a look. The dogs, one a Chow Chow and German Shepherd mix, the other a German Shepherd, attacked Bernice when she tried to pick up one of the three puppies.

As Diana ran for a pole to fend off the dogs, her mother, Sonia, rushed into the yard and jumped on top of Bernice to protect her from the two mad animals. She then scooped up the four-year-old child and ran into a nearby shed in the yard. When the dogs calmed down, she walked out of the yard, and seeing the extent of the wounds to her neighbors' child, she then called the police (*Ft. Lauderdale Sun-Sentinel*, May 6, 1991).

Large German Shepherd dogs, growling, angry, ferocious, jealous, attacking a little four year old, and the woman next door throws herself on top of her to protect her. Not even the child's mother. An expression of "no greater love," for here was a willingness to lay down one's life for another. Here is genuine love expressed. Is there doubt in anyone's mind that this expression of love was selfless, not self-serving in any way? She was willing to sacrifice herself for the benefit of another—Christian love. We stand in awe of it.

A less-dramatic expression was seen in Oswald Goldry, who, in 1940, was an American missionary in China. He was arrested and expelled from that country by the Chinese authorities. Upon leaving China, he journeyed to India to arrange for his return home. Passing through a coastal area of India, he encountered a network of Jewish refugees—most of them living in attics, barns, and tents, and some still looking for shelter. The refugees had fled from Nazi persecution in Germany, and they desperately needed help.

The conditions were such that the missionary was powerless to do much. Nevertheless, he felt that he couldn't just leave without doing something. So he cashed the check he had received for passage home and gave it to one of the refugee families! In due course, his passage was again provided by the Missionary Society, and he returned home. On his return, he was interviewed by a reporter from a religion magazine. During the interview, the reporter's questions led to the details of the missionary's expulsion from China and the trip home, including his contacts with the Jewish refugees in India. "Why did you, a Christian missionary, give your passage money to them?" the reporter asked. "After all, it was all you had, and they don't even believe in Jesus!" "You are right," said the missionary, "but I do" (*Good News*, April, 1991). The relevant matter in genuine love is our motivation. Did we want to better the good of another? Did we act in a way that Jesus would have acted?

Isn't it interesting that Paul had never been to Rome when he wrote them and encouraged them to have genuine love? He had never even received a letter from them asking him any spiritual questions. He had never had an opportunity to solve any of their problems. But, because there were people in that church, he knew people and he knew that people were struggling with the development of genuine love. He assumed correctly that this struggle was a universal human problem for all who desire to be Christians. He was right on target, for now, as well as then, we all wrestle with this challenge.

Our modern culture is so committed to self-service that someone wrote the following humorous prayer: "Now I lay me down to sleep, I pray my Cuisinart to keep. I pray my stocks are on the rise, and that my analyst is wise, that all the wine I sip is white, and that my hot tub's watertight; that racquetball won't get too tough, that all my sushi's fresh enough. I pray my cordless phone still works, that my career won't lose its perks, my microwave won't radiate, my condo won't depreciate. I pray my health club doesn't close, and that my money market grows. If I go broke before I wake, I pray my Volvo they won't take."*

Love is the rainbow upon which the eight colors are spread. "Let love be genuine. . . ." Helen Fazio's expression of love for her imprisoned brother, Joseph Cicippio, was classic. Joseph Cicippio was taken hostage in Lebanon by pro-Iranian Shiites and was eventually held for 5 ½ years. But Helen also had her problems. For 12 years, her ovarian cancer had been in remission, but now she had been informed that it had recurred and she had only two weeks to two months to live.

Fazio, however, defied her prognosis, and with the power that only love can provide, she became the family cheerleader while her family stood vigil during Joseph's captivity. She said she would not die without embracing her younger brother, Joseph, one more time.

*My apologies to the author, whom I could not trace.

On December 5, 1991, Fazio's promise was fulfilled when her brother waded through a throng of TV cameras and reporters to hug his sister inside their brother Thomas's Norristown, Pennsylvania, home. "Oh, Joe! Joe! I love you so!" she said as they embraced for the first time in years. She died five months later (*Trenton Times*, April 24, 1992).

Helen Fazio's death-defying act of love for her brother is a model of what is in store for us when we perform such an act of genuine love for all our brothers and sisters in need around the world.

> *I have said these things to you so that my joy*
> *may be in you, and that your joy may be*
> *complete. John 15:11*

Joy

I s our lack of joy due to the fact that we are
Christians, or to the fact that we are not Christian enough?" Paul Tillich raised this question
in *The New Being* (New York: Charles Scribner's
Sons, 1950, p. 42). I wonder what the answer is? We
sing, "Joyful, Joyful, We Adore Thee . . ." and we call
God the "Giver of immortal gladness. . . ." We sing,
"All thy works with joy surround Thee . . ." and all
these works "call us to rejoice in Thee." We sing that
God is the "Well spring of the joy of living," and we
ask him to "lift us to the joy divine." We sing how
"joyful music leads us sunward in the triumph song
of life."

Are you really as joyful as that hymn seems to indicate? Are those really your feelings or just the feelings
of Henry van Dyke, the author of the words? Maybe
he felt that way, but you do not. "Is our lack of joy due
to the fact that we are Christians, or to the fact that
we are not Christian enough?"

You have heard the story about the worshiper who
was shouting and hollering in the last pew of a church
at various times during the service. After one gleeful

alleluia, the usher rushed up to him and asked, "Is there anything wrong?" "Not at all," he responded, "I've got religion."

"Well," said the usher, "you didn't get it here." Would you be ushered out of church if you were too joyful? Would your cohorts at work usher you out if you were full of joy? Would your classmates at school usher you out if you were joyful on campus? If you were always full of joy, would your spouse wonder what happened to you? If you embraced this fruit of the Spirit, would your personality be so dramatically altered that your everyday acquaintances would think that you have had a serious personality change?

> *"Have your eyes ever watered out of sheer joy in worship?"*

In the Bible, joy is expressed in worship by shouting, by a loud voice, by playing a pipe, harp, trumpet, flute, or stringed instrument. Joy in the Bible is an action of dancing, leaping or stamping our feet. Joy is smiling faces, twinkling eyes, and expectant feelings. Joy is getting all bubbly and feeling the emotions rising up in you, feelings over which you have no control. I had those feelings when I held my grandchild for the first time. I was overwhelmed by joy. Joyful tears filled my eyes. Have your eyes ever watered out of sheer joy in worship? I hope so. I grew up in the House of Hope Church in St. Paul, Minnesota. Every church should be a House of Joy Church. Unashamed, blatant, tearful, outrageous, uninhibited joy! When it isn't, it lacks one of the outward indicators of the presence of the Holy Spirit.

Jesus Christ is a person of joy, for a relationship of love with God leads to joy. Every Sunday school room in this nation should have a smiling Jesus on its walls. Every sanctuary in this nation should have a smiling Jesus looking down upon us. It is a travesty that in most of our minds we do not think of Jesus as smiling when we imagine Jesus. Do you ever think of Jesus with the twinkling eyes?

Jesus is telling us in the Gospel of John that he is the true vine and that we are the branches. We are connected to him for life, and when we are cut off from him we die. We are nothing without him. We are dependent on him for life and sustenance. Jesus said, "Apart from me you can't do a thing" (John 15:5). In our text, Jesus tells us, "I have said these things to you so that . . ." What? . . . "my joy." Jesus wants to share his joy with us. Jesus, the "joy of man's desiring," the joyful Jesus, wants to share his joy with us. Too often we only think of him as rejected and a man of sorrows, but through all he experienced, he was a joyful Jesus. He had a relationship of love with God that led to joy. The author of the book of Hebrews tells us Jesus "for the sake of the joy that was set before him endured the cross, disregarding its shame, and has taken his seat at the right hand of the throne of God" (12:2). Jesus endured all that he endured, not for the fun of it. It wasn't fun. Not for the glory of it. There was no earthly glory. Not for the power in it. There wasn't any. But for the joy that was set before him, the joy of being in the presence of God himself. Being with God, obeying God, doing the will of God on this earth, produces joy in the hearts of human beings. That's what God promises to his faithful people today. He promises all who would obey him pure joy.

> In the cross of Christ I glory,
> Towering o'er the wrecks of time;
> All the light of sacred story
> Gathers round its head sublime.
>
> When the woes of life o'ertake me,
> Hopes deceive, and fears annoy,
> Never shall the cross forsake me.
> Lo! it glows with peace and joy.
>
> When the sun of bliss is beaming
> Light and love upon my way,
> From the cross the radiance streaming
> Adds more luster to the day.
>
> Bane and blessing, pain and pleasure,
> By the cross are sanctified;
> Peace is there that knows no measure,
> Joys that through all time abide.
> —John Bowring, 1825

Abiding joy is to be found in God's presence, because joy is at the very heart and nature of God.

Because Jesus is full of joy from being in the presence of God and from being God, he wants us to be full of joy also. If it is a major travesty that every Sunday school and every sanctuary is not adorned with a smiling Jesus, it is a worse travesty that every person in Sunday school and every person in worship is not smiling, for a relationship to a joyful God through the joyful Jesus leads us to be joyful disciples.

> *Joy is a by-product of a relationship with God through Jesus Christ.*

Our text quotes Jesus as saying, "I have said these things to you so that my joy may be in you, and that your joy may be complete." Other translators refer to "complete joy," "perfect joy," and "your cup of joy will overflow."

Joy is a by-product of a relationship with God through Jesus Christ. The world does not give this relationship and this joy, and so the events of this world cannot take this relationship and this joy away. Now, that's an important point! Happiness comes and goes. Happiness may disappear with the next telephone call. Your loved one dies. Your X ray shows bad news. Your car needs repairs. Your stocks are worth nothing. Your C.D.'s which were insured by the federal government, are not. Sorry about that mistake. There goes your happiness. But your joy is based on a relationship to God through the joyful Jesus, and he will never be taken away. He is always there. "Jesus never fails, never never fails. I'm glad so glad, Jesus never fails."

I begin and end with Paul Tillich: "Is not the decision to be a Christian, a decision for the joy in God instead of the [happiness] of the world?" (*The New Being*, p. 144). I think so! I know so!

> *The peace of God, which surpasses all understanding, will guard your hearts and your minds in Christ Jesus. Philippians 4:7*

Peace

Listen to Richard Brandt's description of the beautiful stained-glass window that is in St. Machar Cathedral in Aberdeen. "High on the rear wall is an impressive colored picture of the disciples and then below each disciple how tradition says they died." None of them died in bed from old age, by the way.

"There is Simon Peter and a picture of his death upon a cross turned upside down. James, the son of Zebedee, is shown and then a visualization of how he was beheaded by Herod Agrippa I. John, the brother of James, perished by being boiled in oil. Andrew was first stoned and then crucified for good measure. Bartholomew was tied up in a sack and thrown into the sea. Matthew was burned at the stake in Rome. Thomas was run through with a spear. Philip suffered crucifixion under the rule of Domitian. James, the son of Alphaeus, was stoned after being pushed from a high wall. Thaddeus met a gruesome death; his head was split open with an ax. Simon, the Zealot, was clubbed to death. Judas hanged himself. Paul was beheaded in Rome."

The scenes of those thirteen disciples and their deaths are placed below the central panel of Christ and his death on the cross. It is a sobering reminder of the kind of hostile reception that the secular world has waiting for a committed Christian. The world is not waiting to offer us peace.

The word *peace* is one of those ambiguous English words. It has many meanings. For some, peace means the cessation of war. For others it means not a worry in the world. It's an important word and it needs defining in the biblical sense, for it is one of the nine fruit of the Holy Spirit about which Paul speaks in his letter to the Church at Galatia. When you have God's presence with you, you will also have peace. What can we say about this peace?

> *"When you are reborn you will have a passionate allegiance to the whole family of humankind."*

Biblical peace is God's peace. The Prince of Peace gives us the message that our family is the whole world. In the Scripture lessons we read how Jesus said that he did not come to bring peace but a sword, not peace but division. Individual members of each family will be at odds with one another over their commitment to Jesus Christ. This Prince of Peace redefines family by saying all humankind is his family: the refugees, the hostages, the hospitalized, the AIDS victims, the lonely, the homeless, and the hungry. Most of us are born with a passionate commitment to our immediate blood families. Jesus is pointing out that when you are reborn you will have a passionate allegiance to the whole family of humankind, which is the whole family of God.

This peace is God's peace for it is given by God, and hence, the world cannot take it away, no matter what happens to you in the world. On Saturday, March 30, 1991, at 3:30 A.M., eight adults and five children pushed their sixteen-foot, blue and white fiberglass boat off the Cuban shore out to sea. Using a tiny compass, they fought high winds, towering waves and hunger for four days after their motor died within sight of the United States. On Wednesday, at 1:45 A.M., they were washed ashore near Hollywood, Florida. Sunburned, blisters on their hands from rowing, dehydrated, hungry, they declared, "We feel so happy to be free." It is astounding what people will endure to get to America and to experience what we take for granted! How were they able to endure such a family ordeal? The eighteen-year-old son gave this answer: "Everyone was seasick. We bailed with our hats, but we were never frightened. It was easy with faith in God." (*Ft. Lauderdale Sun-Sentinel*, April 4, 1991).

Out in the middle of the ocean, tossed to-and-fro by monstrous waves, out of food, small children being burned by the sun, bailing the water with their hats and literally paddling with their hands, they had God's peace, "which," says our text, "surpasses all understanding. . . ." It is hard to understand, isn't it? But we don't have to understand it. All we have to do is believe it and that kind of peace is ours.

This peace, says the Living Bible, will "keep your thoughts and hearts quiet and at rest" (Philippians

4:7). Wouldn't that be wonderful in this disturbing world? Wouldn't that be pleasing to our roller coaster lives? God's peace puts our thoughts at rest. It puts our hearts at rest. This further defines what kind of peace is God's peace. This puts more flesh on the bone of peace, and we realize that one of the gifts of God's Spirit, one of the fruit is going to be a peaceful quiet and a peaceful rest. This is not a rest that is given in a hammock or at bedtime, but a rest that quiets our hearts and thoughts in time of turmoil. This value is a calmness when all around us the world is rioting. This calmness is not produced because we do not understand the situation, but because God has given it to us as a gift, a by-product of having his Holy Spirit in our lives. "Be still and know that I am God!" says the psalmist (46:10). It is a peace that every original disciple had as he died and a peace promised his disciples today.

> "The peace of God is the result of deliverance from self."

The peace the world offers us only offers us deliverance from tribulation; the peace of God is the result of deliverance from self. Worldly peace is made by humans; religious peace is God-given. Neither one is supposed to take the place of the other, but neither is one to be identified with the other. Some may be disappointed in this sermon because I am not denounc-

> ## *"Peace does not belong to anyone."*

ing war or endorsing Greenpeace. I do not see the biblical message leading me in either direction. Biblical peace is God's gift to his people in a fallen, war-mongering world, and since the world does not give this kind of peace, neither can it take it away.

Finally, note that peace is triggered by a "trust in Christ Jesus" (Living Bible). Peace does not belong to anyone. Biblical peace is a by-product of a lifetime commitment to Jesus Christ as your Lord and Savior.

Jesus asked, "Do you think I have come to give peace on the earth?" (Luke 12:51). The world answered a resounding "Yes!"

Not so, says Jesus. I have come to give salvation from your sins and salvation to a more meaningful life. Commit your life to me and receive the gift of the Holy Spirit, and you have biblical peace. As you trust in Christ Jesus you will find your thoughts quieted and your heart at rest, and that is to experience God's peace.

Ernest Campbell tells about the woman who went to a pet store to purchase a parrot to keep her company and to give her some peace. She took her new pet home but returned the next day to report, "That parrot hasn't said a word yet!"

"Does it have a mirror?" asked the storekeeper. "Parrots like to look at themselves in the mirror." So she bought the mirror and returned home.

The next day she was back, announcing that the bird still wasn't speaking. "What about a ladder?" the storekeeper said. "Parrots enjoy walking up and down a ladder." So she bought a ladder and returned home.

Sure enough, the next day she was back with the same story—still no talk. "Does the parrot have a swing? Birds enjoy relaxing on a swing." She bought the swing and went home.

The next day she returned to the store to announce the bird had died. "I'm terribly sorry to hear that," said the storekeeper. "Did the bird ever say anything before it died?"

"Yes," said the lady. "It said, 'Don't they sell any food down there?'" (*Preaching*, March/April 1991, p. 58).

We readily buy mirrors by which to primp, ladders by which we climb higher, swings by which we seek pleasure. But where is the food for our souls?

Jesus Christ is the soul food that gives your thoughts and your hearts quiet and rest, and that is biblical peace, and it will last a lifetime.

"Don't they sell any soul food down there at the church?" "Yes! Yes! It's just that many people aren't buying it."

> *Love is patient. . . . It bears all things, believes all things, hopes all things, endures all things. Love never ends. I Corinthians 13:4*

Patience

"O Lord, I know that I am not yet perfect, and hence, I pray for the gift of patience. Please give it to me right now." The humor of that prayer illustrates the universality of our need for patience. We all need patience, and we are not willing to wait for it.

When I look at Galatians 5:22, I am struck by the difficulty of obtaining these nine fruit of the Spirit. None of them come naturally. As a matter of fact, in most instances, their opposite is what comes naturally. That is how I know that these fruit are gifts from God, and have to be inspired by God to dwell in us. By our nature, we are just the opposite. Or are you naturally loving, naturally kind, naturally peaceful, or naturally patient? These fruit are the by-products of the presence of the Holy Spirit in our lives. They are the fruit of the Spirit, a gift from God.

The Apostle Paul, writing to his protege, in I Timothy 1:12-17 reminds us that God is actually a patient God. As a matter of fact, Paul thinks that God used him as "Exhibit A," as an example of how patient God can be with humankind. We know that Paul, before his conversion to Christ on the Damascus Road, was one who eagerly and aggressively sought out Christians wherever he could find them and had them killed. He wrote, "I hunted down (Christ's) people, harming them in every way I could" (I Timothy 1:13, Living Bible). He was present at, and may have participated in, the stoning to death of Stephen, the first Christian martyr. "But God had mercy on me," Paul wrote, "so Christ Jesus could use me as an example to show everyone how patient he is with even the worst sinners, so that others will realize that they, too, can

> *"God is patient too."*

have everlasting life" (I Timothy 1:16, Living Bible). Other translators refer here to God's "perfect patience," "his inexhaustible patience," "his unlimited patience," and "his full patience," God's patience with us sinners is one of the dominant messages of both the Old Testament and the New Testament. Exodus (34:6-7) proclaims, "The Lord, a God merciful and gracious, slow to anger, and abounding in steadfast love and faithfulness, keeping steadfast love for the thousandth generation." The prophet Nehemiah (9:17) proclaimed, "You are a God ready to forgive, gracious and merciful, slow to anger and abounding in steadfast love, and you did not forsake them."

Second Peter (3:9) in the New Testament says, "The Lord is not slow about his promise, as some think of slowness, but is patient with you, not wanting any to perish, but all to come to repentance." A few verses later (3:15) he says we are to "regard the patience of our Lord as salvation." The whole Bible is telling us that we have a God who is patient. Arthur Ainger (1894) has written in a hymn, "God is working his purpose out as year succeeds to year. . . ." Our God is a patient God.

Our Corinthian text also reminds us of this attribute of God. We know that God is love, and our text from I Corinthians (13:4) seeks to put some specifics on that kind and quality of love by saying, "Love is patient." Following the logic of a syllogism, God is love; love is patient; therefore God is patient. There is little argument here. The need seems to be to persuade humankind that we should therefore be patient people.

> *"Patience means placing the outcome of the situation in someone else's hands."*

I have difficulty with patience because to be patient is to admit that I do not have to do anything, or that I cannot do anything. As a sinner, I want to be in control of my life, my children's lives, my grandchildren's lives, and watch out, maybe even your life. I want to be in control of everything, but to be patient implies inactivity. It means letting someone else do the work. Patience means placing the outcome of the situation in someone else's hands, and that's hard because they may mess it up. It might not turn out the way I want it to turn out. It means that I let go and let God. I guess this is why love "bears all things, believes all things, hopes all things, endures all things" (I Corinthians 13:7).

Our text would imply that being more patient would also make us more loving, and knowing that God is love, more patience would make us more God-like. But it is so hard. Many persons prayed for my grandson, Benjamin. He caught bacterial meningitis after two weeks of life and spent the next fourteen days in the hospital having seizures, high fever, and other difficulties. We count it a miracle to see him alive. When persons inquire about his health, I tell them that the real outcome will be known in about six years. We are told that we have to be patient and wait to see how his little brain and eyes and ears and other little organs develop. We wait to see if, in fact, he has been damaged by this disease, or damaged by the drugs that saved his life. I almost feel apologetic when I respond that we really won't know for sure until he is six years old. We have to be patient.

"But I want to know now! Will he be all right or not? Tell me now, God!" God's answer to me is, "Wait!" My answer, "I can't!" God's answer, "Tough. Love is patient." My answer, "Well, okay, I'll try, but six years! It's not natural." God's answer, "That's right! It's supernatural!"

> *Note then the kindness and the severity of God: severity toward those who have fallen, but God's kindness toward you, provided you continue in his kindness. Romans 11:22*

Kindness

When you are raising four children, as we did, who were less than four years apart from the oldest to the youngest, you will grasp at any straw to maintain order. One of my favorite cliches was not "cleanliness is next to godliness," but "quietness is next to godliness." When there are six of you living under one roof, the coveted value is not cleanliness, but silence.

Another of my favorite "survival quotations" was from the Bible. When one of the children was behaving in a manner less than desirable, I would tell them, "Be ye kind." It was from the King James version of Ephesians 4:32, because I memorized in Sunday school from that version. If I said it once, I must have said it a hundred times, "Be ye kind." I valued kindness then in my children, and I value it now in all of God's children. You never outgrow the need to have this value in your life. This is why the Apostle Paul specifically refers to it as one of the obvious indicators of the presence of the Holy Spirit in a person's life (Galatians 5:22).

David Hubbard wondered out loud, "What is the key to the success of the Los Angeles Dodgers?" Then he answered his own question by saying, "Teamwork. At least that is the answer given in a radio commercial familiar to thousands of Dodger fans . . . But it is no secret to those who follow baseball closely that the famous teamwork has exploded into dissension on several occasions. Two stars fought in the locker room before a game. Another star called one of the Dodger presidents a liar. Spirited American men we call them. They are proud, highstrung, competitive achievers, with a high sense of honor as to how they are treated. For them, achievement and pride go hand in hand. Their coaches, team mates, and fans tolerate all kinds of surly, peevish, abusive, or explosive behavior from players who are valuable to the team."

> *"The church is not oriented to winning at any cost."*

Then Dr. Hubbard, who was the president of Fuller Theological Seminary in Pasadena, California, adds, "As long as the pitcher can hold the other team to two runs in most games, as long as the catcher can throw out the faster runners, as long as the batter can hit .300 and drive in 100 runs per season, behavior does not matter. So it goes in baseball and in much of the rest of life." (*Unwrapping Your Spiritual Gifts*, Waco: Word Books, 1985, p. 117)

That's a scary thought isn't it? I mean, if our behavior does not matter, as long as we are producing, then we might as well close up shop, for the church is not oriented to winning at any cost. Behavior is crucial. Success for us is not numbers, or dollars, but lives changed, and faith deepened.

The shortstop threw the ball to the first baseman in time for a forced out, but the first baseman dropped it. The umpire did not see the first baseman drop the ball, and so he called the runner out, to the surprise of the runner, and to the delight of the first baseman. Now you know an argument is going to ensue. The runner is going to claim that the first baseman dropped the ball and therefore he was safe. Everybody saw that he dropped the ball except the umpire, who was shielded from the play. Wouldn't it be wonderful if the first baseman were to say, "Hey, the runner is right, you know. I did drop the ball. You missed it. You shouldn't have called him out. He was safe." You know what would happen? The first baseman would become the laughing stock of the league. Maybe the nation. Maybe of the world. Behavior doesn't matter. Results matter. Winning matters. Outs matter. It's one of the worldly rules of the game of life.

Christians are in another game of life, an eternal game of life. Our rules, and our goals are different. We live in the world but we do not follow the rules of the world because they are not of eternal value. The values of Galatians 5:22 are the ones that are eternal. It is they that we adhere to. The kind thing to do in that situation would have been to tell the umpire that you, in fact, did drop the ball and the runner is safe. Whether he believes you or not is up to him, but you did the kind thing. You expressed the eternal value, rather than the worldly value. Worldly values end when you leave this world. Eternal values continue on when you leave this world. We leave behind us all of these secular values, but we take with us the eternal ones. Heaven is full of eternal values, and we begin participating in heaven when we embrace the eternal values now. People hoping to go to heaven had better start living out the heavenly values.

Our problem is that we look too often at the values of others and not often enough at God. Allen Dixon wrote, "My father is a TV repairman, and when he comes home he wants to think about something else. My mother often says that everyone's television works right except our own. Since the antenna on top of the house had one arm broken off by a windstorm, it has never supplied as strong a signal as it should.

"Not long ago a new family moved in next door, and soon the man appeared on his roof to install his own antenna. Knowing that my father is a TV technician, he drilled the lead-in hole in the same location, secured the base, and turned the aparatus facing the identical direction as Dad's. Then, studying my father's roof a moment longer, he reached up and, with a yank, broke an arm off his brand-new antenna." (Allen Dixon, Columbus, Ohio, *The Reader's Digest*, November 1977, p. 136). Too often we only look to each other for our values. We do not look high enough.

I imagine that the first baseman who cheats is not always unkind. I would guess that he is selectively unkind. If he is unkind all the time, he would really have no friends, no wife, no family. How could we really stand a person who is always unkind to everyone? We couldn't! His problem is probably that he is kind to some and mean to others, like most of us are.

> *"Selective kindness then becomes a tool, or technique, to manipulate others. It helps us get through the day."*

Selective kindness then becomes a tool, or technique, to manipulate others. It helps us get through the day. We turn it on when it is helpful and turn it off when we don't need it. Such behavior can be seen in the boss who is a stinker to his employees, but a kind husband and father. Such behavior can be seen in law breakers who are ruthless in their criminal behavior, but kind to animals. Such behavior can be seen in some political dictators, like Saddam Hussein, who bombs defenseless Kurds and starves them, but then pats little boys on their heads when the cameras are rolling.

Our text (Romans 11:22) from Paul's letter to the Church in Rome is intriguing because it describes two sides of God: his kindness and his severity. If God were described as only severe, he would be unapproachable. If he were only kind, he would be a marshmallow, a deity with no backbone. The biblical God is one who judges us, who chastises us, who disciplines us, but God judges, chastises and disciplines us with kindness. The severity tempers the kindness and the kindness tempers the severity. For all who continue to be kind, we have the biblical promise that God will likewise be kind, but to all who harden their hearts to God, they will call down upon themselves the severity of God. In this text we see God's harshness on one hand and softness on the other. Justice and mercy belong together.

You will recall that Stephen was one of the early disciples, who when there was complaining that some of the needy were being neglected, was appointed with six others to express the compassion of the Jerusalem Church. He quickly ran into trouble with the local Jewish authorities, and while preaching was interrupted by a furious mob, charged with blasphemy, and stoned to death. Remember one of the approving bystanders? Paul, or Saul of Tarsus as he was then known, may have even picked up a stone. Even today we send forth Stephen ministers to bring good news to the needy, as we heal physical ailments.

"Shortest Sermon Sunday"

John Albrecht, Rector of St. Mary's-in-the-Hills Episcopal Church in Lake Orion, Michigan, wanted to find a special way to mark his little church's twenty-fifth anniversary. At last the idea came to him. If a friend of his had preached the world's longest sermon (No, it wasn't me.)—60 hours and 31 minutes— why shouldn't he preach the shortest sermon?

It sounded easy enough. It wasn't. Distilling the Christian message to that degree was much harder than he had anticipated, even with the help that came to him as parishioners and strangers alike inundated him with one-word suggestions, such as compassion, believe, repent, amen, Lord, peace, brotherhood, Jesus. People stopped him on the street to tell him their ideas. A waitress scribbled something on a brown paper bag and handed it to him while he was eating—"we," it said.

On Shortest Sermon Sunday, it was raining hard, but that didn't keep the crowd from packing the little church to see Father Albrecht advance to the pulpit and spread his arms to the congregation, to hear him utter the single, beautiful word . . . What was it? "Love"—and what is love? "Love is kind" (I Corinthians 13:4).

Goodness

"Train children in the right way, and when old, they will not stray" (Proverbs 22:6). As a child, I was taught the following table grace, and I have not departed from its message:

> God is great and God is good
> Let us thank him for our food.
> By his hands we all are fed.
> Give us Lord, our daily bread.
>
> Amen.

Knowing that God is good from my very early years, I was not surprised to read in the Bible that one of the nine indicators of the presence of the Holy Spirit in one's life is going to be, according to the Good News Bible, the ingredient of goodness. The Apostle Paul, writing to a Church in Galatia, wrote (5:22) that the fruit of the Spirit are love, joy, peace, patience, kindness, goodness (generosity, NRSV), faithfulness, humility (gentleness, NRSV) and self-control. I know these are gifts from on high because they are so hard to cultivate in my own life. None of these come easily. None of us is born with them. They are a gift of God when we commit our lives to Jesus Christ as our Lord and Savior. They are the by-product of that faith.

> *"The goodness of God is generosity because God is choosing to share something out of the divine economy with others who do not have it."*

Note how "goodness" is translated from the Greek word as *generosity* in the Phillips translation, and also in the New Revised Standard Version. I find that very suggestive and consistent with the Scripture lesson from John 10:11-12 and our text from Titus. The goodness of God is generosity because God is choosing to share something out of the divine economy with others who do not have it. God is reaching out to human beings and giving us something that we desperately need. God wants us to benefit from what God has, and so, God generously contributes to our well-being. This good thing that God is sharing with us, according to our text, is the gift of salvation "through the washing of rebirth and renewal by the Holy Spirit." Rebirth and renewal from God for each one of us. What a generous act of a great Person, a good God! "God is great and God is good."

In the Gospel of John (10:11-21) we hear Jesus claiming to be, not just the shepherd, but the good shepherd. He chose to liken himself to someone who

would be good, and then, he proceeded to give goodness a very sharp and clear definition.

> *"Good people sacrifice what they have for others."*

Jesus says that someone who is good is going to be
willing to lay down his life for someone else. Of
course, as soon as he says this, we all gasp because
that is exactly what Jesus did for us. Jesus wants to
make sure that we know that if we think we are going
to be good people, good Christian people, we are also
going to have to be people who are willing to lay
down our lives in service to the needy. That's goodness.

Good people sacrifice what they have for others.
Good people give what they have to others. Good
people share what they have with others. Good people invite others to participate in whatever it is they
are enjoying at the present time. Good people have
sacrifice at the heart of their being and they carry it
with them wherever they are, giving all the time to
others. Sacrificing for ourselves is easy. Sacrificing for
others is goodness.

Tom Morgan asked, "Have you ever seen some of
the really old cowboy movies on television? If you
have, I'm sure that you have noticed how easy it is to
tell the good guys from the bad guys. Everything is
very clear; you don't even have to pay much attention
to the plot. All the good guys wear white hats and all
the bad guys wear black hats.

"When the bad guys aren't robbing banks, they are

starting fights in a saloon and pushing innocent citizens into the horse trough. When the good guys aren't chasing the bad guys, they are teaching the pretty girl's little brother how to break in his new white horse, or stopping the girl's runaway wagon. There is no chance that you will be confused as to who is the good guy and who is the bad guy." (Thomas D. Morgan, *The Pulpit*, May 1968, p. 11).

> *"Goodness includes an intimate knowledge of people."*

Life, however, is more complex. Who is the good guy and who is the bad guy? Most people are wearing gray hats that look white sometimes and black sometimes. In the midst of the moral confusion of our society, and even the moral confusion of the Church, Jesus says, I am the good shepherd. Look at what I do, do what I do, and you will be good also. Be willing at any given time to sacrifice all that you have and are for others, and you will be good, as I am good.

Second, notice that Jesus says that goodness also includes an intimate knowledge of people. How can we develop such an intimate knowledge? By loving people. "I know my own and my own know me, just as the Father knows me and I know the Father," said Jesus (John 10:14). He knows his own because he cares about his own, because he loves his own, because he wants the best for his own.

We have a God who cares enough for us to have visited us in the flesh. One who was born the way we were born. One who lived the way we are living. And one who died as we will one day die. This is the incarnation of God, in the flesh, with us.

Dr. Joel Mattison is a physician who was reminding nurses of their key role in the healing team in the hospital. He wrote, "Do not forget . . . that long after the physician has left the scene, a sometimes silent . . . cast of characters remains . . . do not forget the nurse, not just for her [his] own personal strength or faith, but for what she [he] needs to be strengthened to do herself [himself]. (Dr.) James Stewart was once asked by such a nurse, 'What is the answer to those with questions about personal suffering who know that they will never again be well and without pain and anguish, and who wonder if anyone, even God, cares? What is the answer?' And he replied to the nurses, 'You are.'" (Joel Mattison, *Princeton Seminary Bulletin,* volume XII, number 1, new series 1991, p. 70). The nurse is. The person by the bedside is. The one nearby who is loving, caring, listening, intimately helping, incarnate love, love with flesh on. People who are there when another person needs them are good people, said Jesus.

> ## *"Goodness is global."*

Finally, goodness reaches out in compassion beyond our immediate friends, our immediate neighbors to the whole globe. You know that, but it is so hard to do. Our problem is that we have defined family as our immediate blood relations only, and for this family we would do anything. Some of you are looking forward to giving a sizable inheritance to your own family. You have read the bumper sticker that says, "I'm spending my children's inheritance." Many of you are doing just the opposite. You have worked, and saved, and now you are going to give members of your family a sizable monetary gift. I would like to have you broaden your definition of family to include the family of the whole human race. There are certainly more needs in this broader family than your immediate family has.

Recently I had the privilege of asking the official board if they would accept a $5,000 gift in a Christian will from a woman who wanted to designate it for the hungry of the world. The story behind her generosity was her appreciation of the fact that she never had to go hungry herself in her lifetime, and she wanted to do something when she passed away that would assure that some people in the whole family of God also never went hungry. Her $5,000 gift will be invested, and the earnings will be available in perpetuity in order to feed the hungry. What a wonderful practical expression of goodness, her concern for all people everywhere, not just her immediate family.

Jesus had this concern, and it is the third and final portion of the trilogy that made up his definition of being good. "I have other sheep that do not belong to this fold. I must bring them also, and they will listen to my voice. So there will be one flock, one shepherd" (John 10:16). Goodness recognizes the one family of humankind.

John Oxenham caught this definition of goodness when he wrote in 1908:

> In Christ there is no East or West,
> In Him no South or North
> But one great fellowship of love
> Throughout the whole wide earth . . .
>
> Join hands, then, disciples of the faith,
> Whate'er your race may be.
> All children of the loving God
> Are surely kin to me.

Religious people have been wrestling with the definition of goodness for thousands of years. The Old Testament prophet Micah (6:8) raised the question: "O mortal, what is good . . . ?" Then he answered his own question: " . . . do justice . . . love kindness, and . . . walk humbly with your God." When the Messiah came from God to save all the people in the world, he fulfilled this prophecy by making it a little more practical and explicit. Jesus, in our Scripture lesson, said that goodness will now involve living a sacrificial life and expressing an intimate concern for people all over the world—that's what being good means. When you have it, "surely goodness and mercy shall follow (you) all the days of (your) life, and (you) shall dwell in the house of the Lord for ever" (Psalm 23:6). Goodness will last a long long time and reach into an infinite number of places.

> *What if some were unfaithful? Will their faithlessness nullify the faithfulness of God? By no means! Romans 3:3*

Faithfulness

A t the Air Force Academy an officer said that the cadets coming in over the last few years are bright students, many from nice families, and most of them are good citizens. The only problem, he said, "is that they have no values."

The problem today is we have valueless children, raised by valueless parents, in a valueless society. Or worse yet, in a society that embraces secular values. But now a recent poll indicates that a radical change is stirring in our great country.

An editorial (April 5, 1991) in the *Ft. Lauderdale Sun-Sentinel* declared, "The emphasis in recent decades on selfishness and roughshod scrambling up the job ladder is being replaced by more basic traditional goals in life. Faith in God ranked higher in importance than anything else in their lives by 40 percent of Americans. Second in importance is good health, named by 29 percent in the poll. Third is a happy marriage, 21 percent. Fourth at 5 percent is a 'job that you enjoy.'"

"This," said the editor, "could represent a real

change in the outlook of Americans, a shift from narrow, groping selfishness to the solid values previously associated with this nation." One scholar (Wade Roof, a professor of Religion, University of California, Santa Barbara) called the finding "astounding," and he said it "suggests a reorientation, a cultural shift." America is beginning to reexamine its value system and to embrace the values endorsed in the Bible.

> *"Our God is faithful, trustful, and to be believed."*

On Pentecost Sunday, we celebrate the coming of the Holy Spirit upon the early church. The arrival of the Holy Spirit was the fulfillment of a promise made by Jesus Christ when he announced, "I have said these things to you while I am still with you. But the . . . Holy Spirit, whom the Father will send in my name, will teach you everything, and remind you of all that I have said to you" (John 14:25).

The Greek word translated "faithfulness" in the New Revised Standard Version is translated "fidelity" in the Phillips translation, and "trustfulness" in the Jerusalem translation. If our God is faithful, trustful, and to be believed when he says something, then the early church should have experienced the power of the Holy Spirit visiting them sometime after the crucifixion. Jesus promised this would happen. It finally did happen on the Feast of Pentecost at the Jewish festival celebrating the giving of the Ten Commandments on Mt. Sinai. "When the day of Pentecost had come," wrote Luke in Acts, "they were all together in one place. And suddenly from the heaven there came a sound like the rush of a violent wind, and it filled the entire house where they were sitting. Divided tongues, as of fire, appeared among them, and a tongue rested on each one of them. All of them were filled with the Holy Spirit" (Acts 2:1-4). If we had been at that place, we would have shouted, Our God is a God that is faithful. He can be trusted to do what he said, for Jesus said he would send the Holy Spirit, and he did.

Of course, there are many other biblical references to the faithfulness of God. There are many indications that the biblical God can be counted on. Psalm 40 says, "I have spoken of your faithfulness and your salvation; I have not concealed . . . your faithfulness from the great congregation . . . let . . . your faithfulness keep me safe forever" (Psalm 40:10). Paul, in his letter to the Church at Rome in our text, wondered out loud if the people's unfaithfulness will negate God's fidelity. "What if some were unfaithful? Will their faithlessness nullify the faithfulness of God? By no means!" (Romans 3:3). Paul makes it even clearer in his second letter to Timothy (2:13) when he wrote, "if we are faithless, (God) remains faithful—for he cannot deny himself." It is almost as if God had no choice but to be faithful to us for that is God's essence. To be other than faithful would make him other than the biblical God. To be consistent with the biblical revelation God must remain faithful to God's people, to you and to me. Now, that doesn't mean that God will give us everything that we want. It means that God will fulfill every promise that he has made to us. God can be counted upon to do that. God can be trusted to do that.

Great is Thy faithfulness, O God my Father,
There is no shadow of turning with Thee;
Thou changest not, Thy compassions they fail not;
As Thou hast been Thou forever wilt be.

Great is Thy faithfulness! Great is Thy faithfulness!
Morning by morning new mercies I see;
All I have needed Thy hand hath provided.
Great is Thy faithfulness, Lord, unto me!
(Thomas O. Chisholm, 1923)

Jesus made another promise and again based his own faithfulness upon it. "He began to teach them that the Son of Man must undergo great suffering, and be rejected by the leaders, the chief priests, and the scribes, and be killed, and after three days, rise again" (Mark 8:31). Can Jesus' words be trusted? Is Jesus faithful to his followers? When we gather to celebrate the Sacrament of Holy Communion, we proclaim that Jesus is faithful to us. He did die. He did overcome death. We too shall overcome our death when we place our life in his hands. When we do that, we too are faithful, trustworthy and full of fidelity. We too are godlike, for we will have the presence of God's Holy Spirit in our lives.

Faithfulness does not come easily or naturally to us. Thomas Monaghan knows this. He has a personal fortune worth over one billion dollars as the owner of Domino's Pizza and also the Detroit Tigers. Over the years, he has acquired the world's largest collection of Frank Lloyd Wright artifacts. He now says, "I want to devote the rest of my life to somehow do some good." He admits he wavered from the faith during a tour of duty in the U. S. Marine Corps, but asserts that he has grown more resolute about his religious convictions as he has moved into his middle age.

Monaghan contends that his pizza empire has flourished because the corporate philosophy of his company is the Golden Rule. He concedes that he personally often falls short of the high standards of performance and morality for which he crusades. "I tend to be greedy, selfish, egotistical and lazy," he said. "I want to get to the point where I do what I should, not what I want."

An article in the *Chicago Tribune* said that, after reading C. S. Lewis' *Mere Christianity*, Monaghan came face-to-face with his own prideful instincts—and he blinked. After years of planning a 22,000 square-foot dream house on a twenty-seven acre lot, and about one-third of the way into the construction of the estate, estimated to cost five million dollars, Monaghan ordered work halted while he contended with guilt pangs.

"Pride is a great sin," he said, "and as I read the (C. S. Lewis) book, I came to realize that I was doing all the little things right and all the big things wrong . . . I've been dreaming of this house all my life and I got carried away. It's just not me. It's too much house." (*Ft. Lauderdale Sun-Sentinel*, May 1991).

Thomas Monaghan, no saint, an admitted sinner, struggles to be a rich Christian American, faithful to his Lord and finding comfort again and again at the foot of the Cross, exactly where we find ourselves in our own personal struggle to be faithful.

Humility

When Pope John II visited the United States in 1979, the details and intricacies of the preparation were mind boggling. The planning required precision and thoroughness. Among the detailed preparation accompanying the excitement there were elements of humor. The newspapers reported the following event:

"Church loses throne room."

In Chicago, the nation's largest Roman Catholic archdiocese, officials preparing for the Pope's arrival discovered, to their dismay, that the local papal throne was missing. It is customary in the Roman Catholic Church for each archdiocese to maintain a "throne room" in case of a visit by the Pope. But since a Pope had never visited Chicago, and hope for one ever coming had been abandoned, the throne room in Cardinal John Cody's residence had been turned into a committee room. The week before the Pope's visit, workers were busy reinstalling a platform for the throne. Officials panicked momentarily when no one could remember what happened to the throne. It was finally found, however, with other discards, in a storage room at a nearby Catholic college (Maxie D. Dunnam, *The Communicator's Commentary: Galatians, Ephesians, Philippians, Colossians, Philemon*, p. 275).

This is a good reminder that a church can lose not only the throne room, and the throne, but sometimes the One who is to be seated upon it. Who is enthroned in your church? Who sits on the throne of the individual lives of your congregation? Who is your Lord? Who governs your life? Who controls your way of living and your daily decisions? Whoever is, whoever does is enthroned as the ruler of your life.

The First Church of Philippi was having difficulty with this very issue. Philippi was a very cosmopolitan city. The composition of the church was pluralistic, reflecting the great diversity of the city, with a variety of differing backgrounds, and opinions, and degrees of commitment. Acts 16 gives us some indication of the diverse makeup of this church. For example, Lydia was a Jewish convert from Asia and a wealthy merchant (Acts 16:14); the slave girl (16:16-17) was probably a native Greek with little status and no monetary accumulations; and the jailer that was mentioned as a member of the church was probably a Roman (10:25ff.). With such an inclusive fellowship, unity had been difficult to maintain.

> *"If there is difficulty in getting along with one another . . . then we are refusing the gift of the Holy Spirit."*

Paul wrote this special letter to them in A.D. 62 when he was in jail in Rome awaiting trial before the Emperor. He had Epaphroditus hand deliver the letter, and after thanking them for their gifts, he got straight to the point. Paul, in the first few verses of Philippians 2 encouraged them to be of the "same mind, having the same love, being in full accord and of one mind" (2:1, 2). It is always exciting to see the variety of people to whom the Christian faith appeals. The church includes people of all colors, people of all education, people of all backgrounds, people with a variety of earthly goods, and all ages. The flip side of the rainbow membership of most churches is that sometimes the colors clash, sometimes the colors run on each other, sometimes the colors compete for prominence, sometimes the colors have difficulty getting along with one another. When that happens, we are not in harmony with how Jesus Christ wants his church to be, and when that happens we are refusing the gift of the Holy Spirit. That there is tension in many a church and many a church member over the inclusiveness of its fellowship is not a new issue. The question is how do you deal with such disharmony when it happens. How do you get the "same mind . . . same love" and "full accord"? The Apostle Paul has four specific suggestions for the church in Philippi, and for any church when the wide diversity of its people threatens to cause tensions. All four are different aspects of humility (Galatians 5:22, GNB).

> *"If we really respected each other more than we respect ourselves, we would listen carefully to what the other person had to say."*

Paul suggests first that we "do nothing from selfish ambition or conceit, but in humility regard others as better than yourselves" (2:3). That would surely solve a number of human relation problems in any church, wouldn't it? If every one of us related to the other with an attitude that regarded the other better than we regard ourselves, it would let the hot air out of many an inflated ego. If we really respected each other more than we respect ourselves, we would listen carefully to what the other person had to say. We would encourage the other person to participate, and we would carefully digest all that the other had to offer. But for some people this is difficult. It would mean that the more highly educated would have to hear what the less educated had to offer. It would mean that the wealthy would have to hear what the less affluent were saying. It would mean that the women would listen to the men, and the men to the women, and both would listen to the youth, who would desire to listen to their elders. Because we hold one another in such high esteem, we would treat one another with profound respect, and in humility, seek out the advice of those the world might consider less prepared on the subject than we. It would be an acknowledgment that God is no respecter of persons, and that the gift of God's Holy Spirit is to the whole church, and to each individual member of the church.

This would mean that the goal of an individual Christian would be like the one that Paul encouraged the Roman Church to have when he wrote, "I say to everyone among you not to think of yourself more highly than you ought to think" (Romans 12:3). Paul is speaking here about our pride and our inability to realize that we are all sinners begging for forgiveness before the Cross.

Christian Herter was running hard for reelection as governor of Massachusetts a number of years ago, and one day he arrived late at a barbeque. He'd had no breakfast or lunch, and he was famished. As he moved down the serving line, he held out his plate and received only one piece of chicken. The Governor said to the server, "Excuse me, do you mind if I get another piece of chicken? I'm very hungry. I had to skip breakfast and lunch this morning."

"Sorry, I'm supposed to give one piece to each person," the woman replied.

"But I'm starved," he repeated, and again she said, "Only one to a customer."

Herter decided it was time to use the weight of his office and said, "Madam, do you know who I am? I am the Governor of this very state."

"Do you know who I am?" she answered. "I'm the

lady in charge of giving only one piece of chicken to each person. Move along." (*Preaching*, March/April 1986, p. 44) "Do not think of yourself more highly than you ought to think."

> *"Help your neighbor get the point across."*

Paul's second suggestion on how to humbly get along with one another in church is found in verse four: "Let each of you look not to your own interest, but to the interests of others." Now that would be different, wouldn't it? If you were to come to the next church meeting prepared to help your neighbor get the point across, rather than getting your point across, we would have not only a unique meeting, but you would have a humbling experience, and in the process, you would experience the presence of the Holy Spirit. If each one of us came to meetings, to programs, to worship with an attitude of what can I do for the people I meet today, it would, says Paul, "Christianize" all our gatherings. If no one came with a personal agenda of seeking influence over others, or striving to get their own pet projects approved, it would revolutionize the church. Paul thought it would revolutionize the Philippian Church, and I would suspect that it would revolutionize your church.

It would mean that we would adopt the servant model in our congregation. It would mean that we would follow Jesus' words when he said, "Whoever wishes to become great among you must be your servant, and whoever wishes to be first among you must be slave of all. For the Son of Man came not to be served but to serve, and to give his life as a ransom for many" (Mark 10:43).

When the custodial staff is on vacation this summer, the church officers will be fulfilling their servant role by cleaning the meeting room, emptying the garbage, and tidying up the rest rooms. . . . That's the model of service that Jesus holds out to us. Perhaps the clergy should take over that duty this summer. Doesn't the Pope visit the jail and wash the feet of criminals every Good Friday in order to remind fellow Christians that this is to be the Christian life-style? Isn't this what Jesus did to his disciples' feet in order to model for us what followers of his should be doing? Humility comes when each one of us begins to look out for the interests of the other person. If you have dirty feet, I'll wash them.

Carl Jung told of a man who asked a rabbi, "How come in the olden days God would show himself to people, but today nobody ever sees God?" The rabbi said, "Because nowadays nobody can bow low enough."

Paul also offered a piece of advice that might be marketed today under the title, *How to Be a Successful Biblical Church*. He said, in essence, this: "Look to Jesus." It's almost too simple, isn't it? But "God loves all simple things. For God is the simplest of all," wrote Leonard Bernstein, in "A Simple Song." The Bible tells us that Jesus was a person "who though he was in the form of God, did not regard equality with God as something to be exploited" (Philippians 2:6). Jesus really had the credentials, the pedigree, if you will, to snub all of us! None of us can say that we are one hundred percent God and one hundred percent human being, for we are only one hundred percent human being. But Jesus could have said, "I'm too divine to fool around with those lowly humans. They are always messing around, and they are so immature. I can't believe it! Wars! Violence! Cheating! Lying! Shameful acts with each other! Will they ever shape up?" If anyone has a good reason for not associating with us, God does.

But, says the Bible, God "emptied himself, taking the form of a slave, being born in human likeness. And being found in human form, he humbled himself and became obedient to the point of death—even death on a cross" (Philippians 2:7-8). To be crucified was a humiliating way to die in biblical times. It had a worse stigma than getting the electric chair, though both are capital punishment—for it was a public event, one in which the whole family suffered humiliation. Jesus allowed this to happen to himself. He humbled himself so much that he allowed humankind to nail him to a cross. And yet, he could have called 10,000 angels to rescue him. Jesus was being obedient to his heavenly Father.

Finally, we are told in the Scripture that because Jesus modeled humility for us, and in essence said he would do "whatever it takes to save humankind," God exalted him and "gave him a name that is above every name, so that at the name of Jesus every knee should bend, in heaven and on earth and under the earth, and every tongue should confess that Jesus Christ is

Lord, to the glory of God the Father (Philippians 2:9-11). Jesus Christ is Lord! Jesus' humble behavior has this consequence: People believe in him as their Lord.

Do you recall the intriguing story that surrounds the Roman Emperor Charlemagne's burial? It is said that he asked to be entombed sitting upright on his throne. He asked that his crown be placed on his head and his scepter in his hand. He requested that the royal cape be draped around his shoulders and an open book placed in his lap.

That was A.D. 814. Two hundred years later Emperor Othello was determined to see if the burial request had been carried out. He allegedly sent a team of men to open the tomb and make a report. They found the body just as Charlemagne had requested. Only now, nearly two centuries later, the scene was gruesome!

The crown was tilted, the mantle moth-eaten, the body disfigured. But open on the skeletal thighs, seated on the throne, was the book Charlemagne had requested—the Bible. One bony finger pointed to Matthew 16:26, his message to us today. "What will it profit them if they gain the whole world, but forfeit their life?" (Max Lucado, *The Applause of Heaven,* Word Books, 1990, p. 153).

> *God did not give us a spirit of cowardice but a spirit of power and of love and of self-discipline.*
> II Timothy 1:7

Self-control

*T*his sermon is based on a proverb. As a matter of fact, it is a biblical proverb: "Like a city breached, without walls, is one who lacks self-control" (Proverbs 25:28). In biblical times a wall built around the city was for the protection of the city. Under siege, the community would retreat behind the wall and defend themselves from the aggressors. If they had no walls, they would have no defense. They were doomed. Their lives would be hopeless and without a future. There would be no protection. So is a person who is out of control, who lacks self-control.

The book of Proverbs also says "It is better to have self-control than to control an army" (16:32, Living Bible). Controlling things outside of ourselves is of little consequence if we cannot keep ourselves under control. If we control everything but ourselves, we still control very little. We are still defenseless, still vulnerable, still hopeless, still doomed, still bound for great difficulty. That's what the Bible says.

> "The discipline of self, the control of human desires . . . is shallow."

In early Greek secular thought the desire for self-control was very much revered. The discipline of self, the control of human desires, usually sexual, was considered a value to be honored. Self-mastery, the ability to get a grip on oneself, was considered admirable by most secular Greeks. To achieve a desirable goal, everyone realized that you must first make sure that you yourself were not out of control. Control yourself, improve yourself, enhance your own skills and abilities, and then you will be able to achieve success. Success was achieved through the discipline of self.

Today's human potential movement would be in full accord with this philosophy. In order to be all that you were meant to be, you must first bring yourself under control, they believe. Plan your work, and then work your plan. Plan ahead. Define your goals for the year, and then measure your performance against those goals. Discipline your way to success.

I don't really know how you can be opposed to this. Proverbs endorses it. Greek culture embraced it. The secular world endorses it. There is really very little wrong with it, except that it is shallow. It needs depth. It never rises above the level of human power. It may bring forth our human potential, but that is all. It organizes us for mental activity, and physical action, but that is all. It leaves out the spiritual dimension altogether. That is the fatal flaw in the human potential movement and in all positive thinkers who leave out God.

When God gives us the Spirit it will be a Spirit of boldness and it will come with "power, and love and self-control," says our text (II Timothy 1:7). The secular world values self-control, but the Christian utilizes it not for personal fulfillment but the glory of God. The world affirms that it is an effective way of accomplishing many desired goals. The world says the self being in control is central, but the Christian says God being in control of self is central. Therein lies the difference between the secular world and the Christian. One utilizes self-control for human potential; the other utilizes self-control for the glory of God.

> "We are saved for a reason; saved for service."

Peter makes it clear that you should "make every effort to support your faith with goodness . . . knowledge . . . self-control . . . endurance . . . godliness . . . and mutual affection" (II Peter 1:5-7). He would agree, I'm sure, that faith in Jesus Christ as our Lord and Savior is enough to save us, but we claim that we are saved for a reason; saved for service. We are saved for a divine purpose. We are not saved so that we can have a life of ease. Jesus didn't have a life of ease. Few Christians really have a life of ease.

Peter assumed that after faith must come effort. "Make every effort" to obtain self-control. He doesn't say it will come easily. He just said pursue it. Our faith needs the support of self-control.

Second, Peter said these things will "keep you from being ineffective and unfruitful . . . For anyone who lacks these things is nearsighted and blind, and is forgetful of the cleansing of past sins" (1:8, 9). Now this is some very practical advice. No one wants to be ineffective in his Christian faith. How can we guard against such a disaster? Control yourself! Be disciplined in your faith and in your practice. Organize your prayer life. Be regular in worship. Be systematic in your giving of money. Share yourself with others in need in a planned stewardship of life. Be in control of your life for the glory of God, and it will be very fruitful and effective. How do I know? The Bible confirms it!

> *"Of all the disciples Peter, himself, was . . . the most undisciplined."*

Third, we notice that Peter is again reminding them of their humanity. He says that they do know what to do and how to do it, but in most instances they simply need to get organized and to get going. "Therefore," he wrote, "I intend to keep on reminding you of these things, though you know them already, and are established in the truth that has come to you. I think it right, as long as I am in this body, to refresh your memory . . ." (II Peter 1:12, 13). I can just see some recipient of this letter thinking, "refresh my memory? What Peter is doing is nagging me to death. Get off my back, fellow. Refresh your own memory!"

Of all the disciples, Peter himself was probably the most intemperate, the most hot tempered, maybe even the most undisciplined. On more than one occasion, he lost his cool. He shouted at Jesus, "Even though I must die with you, I will not deny you" (Matthew 26:35). And then he did. On another occasion when the armed soldiers came to capture Jesus, he jumped into the middle of the fray and cut off the ear of one of the guards (John 18:10). Hot tempered Peter is now telling me to be cool. The kettle is calling the pot black. He should learn self-control. But that's the point. He finally has and that is why it is so instructive coming from him now. He sees now how much more he could have accomplished for the Lord if he had been more disciplined. Life is meant to be disciplined.

In the movie, "Bang the Drum Slowly" by Robert DeNiro there is a symbol of undisciplined living portrayed in a game where the players change the rules as they go along. In this film, members of a baseball team regularly pulled off a bush-league scam on unsuspecting fans. Players would begin a card game in a hotel lobby. Soon fans would sidle up, wanting to be close to the players, and eventually one would ask, "Whatcha playin', fellas?"

"Tegwar."

"Tegwar! Haven't played it before."

"Hey, no problem. Have a seat. We'll teach you." And with that and a few dollars to place on the table, the thrilled fan was in the game. What happened then was merciless. The players would milk the fan for all his money by writing the rules as they went.

"Oh, too bad!" one of the players would say, scooping up the pot. "My one-eyed jack always beats a red ace east of the Mississippi. You must be used to western rules."

"Tegwar," you see, stands for "The Exciting Game Without Any Rules." People with good sense don't join such enterprises, and yet some people live their lives without any rules, out of control.

The National Society of Fund Raising Executives at a national meeting in San Antonio, Texas, recognized the 1991 outstanding philanthropist of the year. Her name wasn't Trump, or Rockefeller, or Bass, but Ethel Hawkins and she was honored for giving more than half of her income to others in 1990.

Mrs. Hawkins is from Pine Bluff, Arkansas, a retired teacher and a widow of a Presbyterian minister. Over the years, she has disciplined herself so that she has given nearly $100,000 to missions, educational programs, and church development. One of her favorite projects is the Heifer Project International, to the sum of $32,000. She has also made contributions to her alma maters, Barber Scotia College and Johnson C. Smith College, and also to the Presbyterian Foundation. In the process she has also helped to start six new churches in Arkansas and North Carolina. In receiving her award, Mrs. Hawkins said, "I gratefully accept this award. I am pleased to receive it, but I am even more pleased if I can challenge others to help, and give, not just financially, but also their service and entire life as the Creator has prospered them.

"I deprived myself of many things in order to share with others—yet they were not missed. The Holy One said, 'Inasmuch as you have done it unto one of the least of these my brethren, ye have done it unto me'" (*National Christian Reporter,* May 17, 1991).

"God did not give us a spirit of timidity, but a spirit of power and love and self-control." Ask Ethel Hawkins, for she knows. Today she says, "What more should one expect but the joy and peace of mind that comes from the Holy Spirit as we share?"

Not only is Ethel Hawkins the 1991 example of outstanding philanthropist of the year, but the 1991 outstanding example of self-control.

> *Therefore, since we are surrounded by so great a cloud of witnesses, let us also lay aside every weight and the sin that clings so closely, and let us run with perseverance the race that is set before us. Hebrews 12:1*

Surrounded by an Orchard

hapter eleven of the book of Hebrews is a roll call of those who lived by faith. It is inspiring to read and to recall their exploits. It speaks of Abel, Enoch and Noah, Abraham, Sarah, Isaac, Jacob, Joseph, and Moses. It speaks of David, Samson, Samuel, and three others, Rahab, Barak and Jephthah, as well as all "the people who crossed the Red Sea" and "the prophets." It speaks of women who received their dead but still believed in the resurrection, and of those tortured, humiliated, imprisoned, stoned, ill-treated, sawn in two, "of whom the world was not worthy." It is simply amazing what a difference faith in God can make in the life of an individual! When one's faith ripens, one becomes a different person.

Here is a litany of the faithful who found themselves in ordinary circumstances but made them extraordinary events by living out their ripe faith on a daily basis. The author of the book of Hebrews makes it clear what made these ordinary people extraordinary when he said, by way of introducing each of them, "by faith." It is almost as if that were their first name. "By faith" Abel, "by faith" Enoch, "by faith" Noah, "by faith" Abraham, "by faith" Sarah. Wouldn't it be wonderful to have your life story introduced in that manner? "By faith" Tom, "by faith" Jan, "by faith" George, "by faith" Joan. How thrilling to be introduced in that manner.

Hebrews 12 is written in response to this litany of the ripe faithful who lived out their lives "by faith." When I listen to a sermon, I always have this question in the back of my mind, "So what?" I grew up asking preachers that question when I heard them preach. Every Sunday when the sermon came I would always respond, "So . . ." I wanted to know what difference the ideas would make in my life. I wasn't being a wiseacre. I was just being practical. I thought then, and think now, that a sermon is not meant to be a theological treatise on how many angels can dance on the head of a pin. I want to know what difference a biblical truth is going to make in my life today. As I read chapter 11, that little question once more appeared in the back of my mind. "So what if all of those women and men had faith? So what?"

Our text answers that question by saying, "Therefore, since we are surrounded by so great a cloud of witnesses, let us also lay aside every weight and sin that clings so closely, and let us run with perseverance the race that is set before us, looking to Jesus the pioneer and perfecter of our faith, who for the sake of the joy that was set before him endured the cross, disregarding the shame, and has taken his seat at the right hand of the throne of God" (Hebrews 12:1, 2). We are surrounded by a great orchard of ripe believers.

> *"We are surrounded by this great cloud of . . . cheerleaders."*

Our text assumes that we who are living today are actually surrounded by all those who ever committed their lives to the living God. The model seems to be an athletic event where we have entered the arena to run the race of life, using Jesus as our inspiration, and we looked up in the stands and there were the millions of others, who at one time placed their lives in God's hands, and who were successful runners in this race of life. How thrilling it is to know that they are there cheering us on! How eager that makes us want to get on with our life, for they have successfully completed the course and they now surround us in order to help us.

How encouraging it is to know that many of them have come through great difficulty, and they never lost their faith. How comforting it is to know that in spite of great adversity, they did not lose their religion. Some of them were martyred, some tortured. We, today, are encircled by the greatness of the past. We are surrounded by this great cloud of witnesses. They are our cheerleaders.

Hebrews emphasizes this, for the author wrote,

"exhort one another every day . . ." (Hebrews 3:13), and he also encouraged us to consider "not neglecting to meet together . . . but encouraging one another" (Hebrews 10:25). He felt the presence of believers would strengthen believer's faith.

Edward R. Murrow described the secret of Britain's stand against the Nazi tyranny by calling it a courage that came less from logic than faith. He wrote, "Unconsciously they dug deep into their history and felt that Drake, Raleigh, Cromwell, and all the rest were looking down at them, and they were obliged to look worthy in the eyes of their ancestors."

When Napoleon was seeking to motivate his tired, dispirited troops in Egypt fighting almost in the very shadows of the great pyramids of that land, he said to his men, "Remember, forty centuries are looking at you."

This is what our text is telling us. Remember, today, you are not alone. Forty centuries of faithful believers surround you.

> *"Some are ripe and some are in the process of ripening."*

How exciting, how comforting, how inspiring that so many people of great faith are watching us today . . . Abraham, Isaac, Jacob, Joseph, Sarah, but you know there are three people in that list who, if you knew who they were, you'd be surprised. I'm speaking of Rahab, the harlot; Barak, a vicious warrior; and Jephthah, the son of a prostitute, who led a band of marauding outlaws, and who killed his own daughter. These all add to David's story, who we know as a "man after God's own heart," who was an adulterer and a murderer, but also one who turned his life around. Some of these clouds of witnesses are listed for their strength. Some are listed for the weaknesses they overcame. Some of them are pretty dark clouds, but who eventually became silver linings.

It's a good reminder that those who God calls are always a mixed bag. Some are ripe and some are in the process of ripening. The followers of God who live by faith include every race, every geographical area, every handicap, every background that there is in the world, because God has created us all, and he calls us all to follow him in Christ. When we do, this "great cloud of witnesses" becomes even more diverse, and it is wonderful.

> *"Look to Jesus."*

A dramatic example of this can be seen in a church in California where Paul is a pastor, a former policeman, and Jeb, a man who spent some time in jail, is a co-pastor. An article in the local paper was titled, "Pastors In Church Are Ex-Cop and Ex-Con." See how the cloud of witnesses is inclusive? Aren't we glad it is?

Finally, the diverse cloud of witnesses is there cheering us on to be more like Jesus, for our text encourages us to "look to Jesus." That is our race in life, to conform more to the life of Jesus. To love more, like Jesus did. To sacrifice more, like Jesus did.

To be as compassionate as Jesus. To be as understanding as Jesus. To be as forgiving as Jesus. To be willing to lay down our lives for another person. This should be our goal in life. To obtain more fruit of the Spirit by "looking to Jesus." To grow ripe.

Have you other goals? If you do, they should be subordinate to this one. The cloud of witnesses is there to encourage us to run the race of life by glorifying the biblical God. Our goal is not to cross the finish line, but to cross the finish line "Looking to Jesus." The "great cloud of witnesses" that surrounds us cheers when our life reflects the glory of the Christlike God. In long distance running, the goal is not so much to be first, but to simply finish. The goal is not to win, but to complete the race and obey the rules during the race. This is our goal in the race of life. Not to be first, but to cross the finish line while glorifying God. The poet and hymn writer wrote:

> Take time to be holy, The world rushes on;
> Much time spend in secret With Jesus alone;
> By looking to Jesus, Like Him thou shalt be;
> Thy friends in thy conduct His likeness shall see.

> Take time to be holy, Let Him be thy Guide,
> And run not before Him, Whatever betide;
> In joy or in sorrow, Still follow thy Lord,
> And looking to Jesus, Still trust in his Word.
> (William D. Longstaff, 1890)

Thomas Chisholm put it this way in 1917:

> Living for Jesus a life that is true,
> Striving to please Him in all that I do;

Yielding allegiance, glad-hearted and free,
This is the pathway of blessing for me . . .

Living and looking to Jesus.

The *Catholic Digest* carried the story of Phillip Kelley, a Franciscan Brother stationed in New Jersey. He was working with Puerto Rican migrant workers who had come to pick tomatoes for Campbell's Soup, vegetables for Bird's Eye, and just about every blueberry you have ever eaten. Many of these workers brought their families. Everyone's dream was to earn enough money to build a house back on the island.

Walter Jansen was retiring after forty years with the canning company; for the past twenty-five years he had been the factory foreman. How he loved the people he worked with! And how they loved him.

Every December, the two hundred Puerto Rican families in the parish would gather, and each family would place five dollars in the pot—about a day's pay for a fruit picker then—and write his own name on a slip of paper. Then someone would be blindfolded and draw the name of the family that would go home for two glorious weeks on the island.

"Why don't you come to the drawing?" Walter suggested to Father Kelley. "I'll introduce you to everyone."

Father Kelley wrote later, "I can still see the paper streamers strung from the rafters under the roof. I can still see on the wall the travel posters of Puerto Rico."

By three o'clock each family had parted with five

dollars. But before the drawing, the announcer called Walter up and presented him with a plaque commemorating his service and expressing their gratitude for his years of care and friendship. Everyone applauded like mad. Then Father Kelley was asked to draw the name of the lucky family.

"On went the blindfold, and I was led to the drum. I reached in, sorted out a handful of entries, and finally settled on one. I took off the blindfold and read the slip of paper: 'Walter Jansen!' The cheers were deafening. Everyone surrounded him, congratulating him, hugging him.

"While the commotion continued down on the floor, I casually reached back into the drum and drew out a handful of slips. Each one, in different handwriting, carried the name—Walter Jansen."

You are surrounded by a great cloud of faithful witnesses, they have all placed your name on their ballot, and now they are all cheering for you.

> *Well done good and trustworthy slave; you have been trustworthy in a few things; I will put you in charge of many things; enter into the joy of your master.* Matthew 25:21

Ripening & Reproducing

Jesus tried to be as clear as possible. He wanted to communicate the good news in such a manner so that no one would misunderstand. Everyone loves a good story, so he told the parable of the talents.

A man went on a long journey and he left his servants in charge. To one he left five talents; to another, two; and to another, one. When the master returned, he called his servants together in order to hold them responsible for the handling of their talents. He wanted an accounting. Fair enough!

Each of the first two had doubled their talents by putting them to work, and the master commended them. The third, however, buried his single talent in the ground, dug it up, and gave it back to the master, safe and secure. The master was furious, grabbed the talent from him, and gave it to the man with five.

What's the message that Jesus wants us "ripe Christians" to garner from this parable? In some ways the message seems unfair, but then whoever promised us that life would be fair? God didn't make that promise.

> ## "We each produce different fruit."

First, Jesus is acknowledging that all of us are created with different abilities, skills, and talents. To say this, is to say the obvious. Sometimes even identical twins are not really identical, much less all the people in the human race. Each one of our fingerprints is different, which ought to tell us something. Each one of our experiences is unique. Children reared in the same family all turn out differently. Each one of us was created to be different from everybody else, and instead of fighting over these differences, we ought to be celebrating these differences.

Some of us are large and some small, some female and some male, some older and some younger, some talkative and some quiet, some black, some brown, some yellow, some red, and some white. Each of us is a special person with different talents. This parable acknowledges, first thing, that we all will have different talents; we each produce different fruit. That's the way God made human beings.

I like this parable because the number of talents that I have is irrelevant. Few of us have all the fruit of the Spirit. The test comes in what you do with what you have been given. Sad to say that sometimes the one-talent person spends too much time moaning over the fact that he has only one talent. He spends too much time wishing that he had more talents, coveting them, rather than using the one that he does have. She spends her days playing a game called, "If only . . . if only . . . if only . . . if only . . ." Then that becomes her excuse for all her mistakes, errors, and defeats in life.

The message of Jesus is clear. We are each different, and differently gifted, and differently fruited. It is all a part of God's plan. Variety is beautiful. You can still be a beautiful Christian without all nine fruit of the Spirit. God has created a rainbow of different people, and it is this variety that we should enjoy and celebrate in life.

A second message from the parable is that whatever you have been given is only validated when it is put in service for Christ. A ticket for a trip is no good until it is put in service. A plane is no good until it is flown. A car is no good if it does not provide transportation. A ballet dancer who cannot dance is not a ballet dancer, and a fruit tree has not performed according to its purpose until it brings forth fruit. Everybody on this earth has been created by a loving God for a purpose.

> *"Our specific calling is to be in warfare with evil. Now I know that bellicose language is not politically correct in the 1990s."*

Each of us has a unique destiny. Each of us is here to reflect, like a mirror, however dimly, God's love. When we do, our reason for being is validated. When we do, our purpose on earth has been fulfilled. The size of the mirror is irrelevant. No matter how many abilities we have, we should put all of them at the service of our Lord and Master.

The Christian Church is called to be in mission here and everywhere in God's world. Our specific calling is to be in warfare with evil. Now I know that bellicose language is not politically correct in the 1990s, but it is the language of the Bible, and especially many of our most beloved hymns. "Fight the good fight with all thy might . . ." "A Mighty Fortress is our God." "Onward Christian soldiers, marching as to war . . . forward into battle, see His banners go . . ." "Stand up, stand up for Jesus, ye soldiers of the cross . . ." "The Son of God goes forth to war, a kingly crown to gain . . ." "Soldiers of Christ, arise, and put your armor on . . ." Part of the difficulty with the Christian Church today is that we do not acknowledge that we are engaged in warfare. Many of our new hymnbooks have intentionally deleted whole hymns, or whole lines like, "And when the strife is fierce, the warfare long . . ." No wonder we are losing this battle with evil. Many do not even know we are at war, or who is the enemy.

For this kind of battle with the forces of evil, we need the kind of commitment that Tim Bowden spoke of in his book, *One Crowded Hour*. In Borneo, in 1964, during a confrontation between the forces of Malaysia and Indonesia, a group of Gurkhas from Nepal were asked if they would be willing to jump from transport planes into combat against Indonesians, if the need arose. The Gurkhas had the right to turn down the request because they had never been trained as paratroopers.

Bowden wrote, "Now the Girkhas usually agreed to anything, but on this occasion they provisionally rejected the plan. But the next day one of their NCO's sought out the British officer who made the request and said they had discussed the matter further and would be prepared to jump under certain conditions.

"The Gurkhas told him they would jump if the land were marshy, or reasonably soft with no rocky outcrops, because they were inexperienced in falling. The British officers considered this, and said that the dropping area would almost certainly be over jungle, and there would not be rocky outcrops, so that seemed all right. Was there anything else?

"Yes . . . They wanted the plane to fly as slowly as possible and no more than 100 feet high. The British officer pointed out the planes always did fly as slowly as possible when dropping troops, but to jump from 100 feet was impossible, because the parachutes would not open in time from that height. 'Oh,' said the Gurkhas, 'that's all right then. We'll jump with parachutes anywhere. You didn't mention parachutes before!'"

That's commitment to a mission, and any church could use this Gurkha-like commitment in its battle against evil, no matter what, in all kinds of weather, under all circumstances, with or without parachutes.

Notice that within the good news, there is bad news if we don't use our God-given talents in service to God. Scholars think Jesus aimed this parable, and especially the condemnation of the one-talent person who buried his talent, at the scribes and Pharisees who viewed their role as one who should conserve and protect what they already had, the Law. They were not willing to risk anything. They wanted to protect their earnings and build a fence around the Law. Hide it. Guard it. Protect it. Bury it.

> *"The matter of reproducing fruit has much to do with one's life-style."*

This was not Jesus' view of how God operated in God's world. God is one who is on the growing edge of life. God is one who wants his followers to launch out with new and exciting avenues of service. God is open to the future and to the risks that the future holds. Jesus didn't like the fact that a religious person would live one's whole life conserving his gains, hiding her assets, burying her talents, not producing fruit. The safe life buries itself in its own well-being, surrounding itself with the good things in life, and safety was simply not a high priority with Jesus.

The matter of reproducing fruit has much to do with one's life-style. How are you using your religious experience? What difference is your faith making in the way you live every day? The number of your talents is irrelevant. How many of the fruit of the Spirit you possess doesn't matter. How you are using them is critical. The one who buried his talent said he did it because, "I knew that you were a harsh man, reaping where you did not sow, and gathering where you did not scatter seed." Jesus is not saying that God is like that. He is suggesting that this is the perception of God that the one has, who hides himself from life. God is a tyrant, he thinks. This person, says our parable, is afraid. "So I was afraid, and I went and hid your talent in the ground" (Matthew 25:25). Those who are afraid of life are afraid in life and therefore they have a religion without any adventure. They have a religion with a closed mind, and those with closed minds could not possibly grasp the idea of God visiting the earth in Jesus Christ. They could not possibly grasp the ideas of a Savior who was a suffering servant. They could not possibly be open to the idea that the Savior of the world would die on the cross and on the third day rise from the dead, and in the process, defeat death for all who will place their life in His hands. Don't confuse me with the facts. I'm going to bury my head along with my talents in the ground. I'm afraid.

Various translators record Jesus as responding by saying, "You lazy rascal!", and calling him "wicked and lazy," ". . . slothful," "bad," and "worthless." I don't think Jesus wants us to act like that, do you? Those are not good words. I hope my behavior does not elicit such a rebuke from my Lord, and I hope yours does not either.

Finally, notice the reward the good people get who put their talents and their lives to work for God. These are called "good and trustworthy," "faithful," "sound and reliable," and "excellent." Now I would like to hear my Lord say that to me. That would be music to my ears. Just to hear those words of encouragement from Jesus would really be enough of a reward. I'd settle for any one of those words. I don't even need to hear them all. Just one of them, Lord, just one. Any one. I'm not even fussy about which one.

> *"We who handle our God given responsibility in a way that is pleasing to God are going to receive (ready for this?) more responsibility."*

But the Lord has an additional reward for those of us who are faithful. According to Matthew 25:14-30, the winner gets an additional trophy. Those of us who take the gifts God has given us and put them in God's service are going to receive something even better than all of those nice words.

We who handle our God given responsibility in a way that is pleasing to God are going to receive (ready for this?) more responsibility. That's what you can expect—more responsibility. "You have been trustworthy in a few things, I will put you in charge of many things; enter into the joy of your master" (Matthew 25:21). Isn't that wonderful? Doesn't that make you joyful? Isn't that better than winning the lottery? It's even better than hearing from the Publishers Clearing House. Your reward for faithfulness in life is more responsibility, more work. The reward for ripening fruit is the opportunity for developing and reproducing more ripe fruit.

Why do I get the feeling that this is not what you had expected, or hoped for? Yet the logic of it is not unfamiliar to us. Many salespeople are working night and day in order to be recognized for their good work so that they might receive a promotion, and in the process, receive more work with added responsibility. Their reward is more responsibility and more work. "Well done, good and trustworthy employee." That will certainly make them joyful.

A good football player works hard all week at practice so he can play on Saturday and work harder at the game. The whole team works hard so that it might play in a Bowl or be in the playoffs. Their reward is more responsibility and more work. "Well done, good and faithful football player." How silly it would be if the football coach came to a player and said, "Son, you have had a good week of practice and I've noticed how hard you have worked and how productive you have been; I'm going to reward you with a well-earned rest this weekend. You deserve it. Here's a ticket to the game. Go and sit in the stands. You'll really enjoy it, for you can see the whole game from this seat, better than if you were in the game, and you can see the half-time activities—the bands, the twirlers, the cheerleaders, and all the celebrities. Congratulations, son, you earned this rest." Why, if that happened, we'd think the coach had been nipping on the "little brown jug."

This line of thinking is also true to this parable and to the theology of the Bible. If you have done a good job, if you have been a faithful Christian, if you have pleased the Lord, if you developed the fruit of the Spirit in your life so that they are ripe, then you have won, not a rest, but a larger opportunity for service, and the chance to grow more fruit of the Spirit. You will be given new challenges. You will benefit from another chance to grow even more, and ripen more in your faith. You will be sent out on another adventure. You will be asked to take new risks, and if you again complete all of these faithfully, you can count on being rewarded again with some more new opportunities for Christian growth, because that's why you are on this earth—to grow in the love of the Christlike God and to be more Christlike yourself, to be ripe fruit of the Spirit.